WRITE
WHAT
YOU'RE
AFRAID
TO SAY

WRITE WHAT YOU'RE AFRAID TO SAY: DANGEROUS WRITING PROMPTS FOR UNLEASHING YOUR AUTHENTIC VOICE by Evan Alkerman

Cover Design by: Diane Brown
Alkerman, Evan – Write What You're Afraid To Say

REFERENCE/Writing Skills

THIS ISN'T AN ORDINARY WRITING PROMPTS BOOK.

THIS IS A BOOK OF DANGEROUS QUESTIONS DESIGNED TO HELP YOU DISCOVER YOUR AUTHENTIC WRITING VOICE. EVERY QUESTION IS LASER FOCUSED ON WHAT MAKES YOU HUMAN.

WHETHER YOU WRITE COMEDY OR DRAMA, FICTION OR NON-FICTION, NOVELS OR MEMOIRS, SONGS OR SCREENPLAYS, *WRITE WHAT YOU'RE AFRAID TO SAY* WILL TAKE YOUR WRITING TO PLACES YOU DIDN'T KNOW WERE THERE.

THESE PROMPTS AREN'T FOR THE MASSES.

YOU'RE ABOUT TO UNLOCK THE SECRET TO WRITING THAT'S:
DARING
FIERY
&
RAW

"I THOUGHT, 'WHAT DO I REALLY WANT TO SAY THAT I'M AFRAID TO SAY?'"
- LOUIS C.K.
(2010 GEORGE CARLIN TRIBUTE)

WHAT DO YOU FEAR THAT YOU THINK NO ONE ELSE FEARS?

WHAT DO YOU THINK ABSOLUTELY NO ONE WOULD AGREE WITH YOU ABOUT?

WHEN WAS THE LAST TIME YOU WERE WRONG ABOUT SOMETHING BIG?

WHAT WAS THE LAST THOUGHT YOU WERE ASHAMED TO HAVE HAD?

WHAT MOMENT MADE YOU REALIZE THAT YOU'RE NOT THE PERSON YOU THOUGHT YOU WERE?

IF YOU LOOKED CAREFULLY, HOW MANY WONDERFUL MOMENTS HAPPENED TODAY?

WHAT WAS THE LAST THING YOU SAID THAT MADE SOMEONE CRY?

HOW DO YOU FEEL DURING YOUR FIRST MOMENT OF CONSCIOUSNESS IN THE MORNING?

WHEN YOU WERE A CHILD, WHAT DID YOU LIKE MOST ABOUT YOURSELF?

WHEN WAS THE LAST TIME YOU PANICKED BECAUSE YOU COULDN'T REMEMBER SOMETHING?

WHAT DO YOU DO IN THE MORNING THAT YOU WOULD NEVER ADMIT TO ANYONE?

WHAT WAS THE LAST DISEASE THAT YOU CONVINCED YOURSELF YOU HAD?

HOW DO YOU FEEL WHEN YOU'RE TRAPPED IN A CONVERSATION WITH SOMEONE?

WHAT IS THE LAST THING YOU WOULD WANT YOUR MOM TO KNOW ABOUT YOU?

WHEN WAS THE LAST TIME YOU HAD AN OPPORTUNITY TO DO SOMETHING GOOD AND YOU MISSED IT?

WHEN HAVE YOU BEEN PROUD OF YOURSELF FOR NO GOOD REASON?

WHEN WAS THE LAST TIME YOU FELT SUPERIOR TO SOMEONE?

WHEN WAS THE LAST TIME YOU FELT INFERIOR TO SOMEONE?

WHAT HAVE YOU NOT STOPPED WORRYING ABOUT SINCE YOU WERE A CHILD?

WHAT DID IT FEEL LIKE THE SECOND TIME YOU FELL IN LOVE?

WHAT DID IT FEEL LIKE THE FIRST TIME YOU FELL OUT OF LOVE?

WHAT MAKES YOU FEEL LIKE YOU'RE GOING CRAZY?

WHAT DID YOU *REALLY* WANT TO SAY IN THAT LAST CONVERSATION WITH A STRANGER?

WHAT IS THE BAD THING YOU THINK ALL THE TIME?

WHERE DOES YOUR MIND GO WHEN YOU'RE DRIFTING OFF TO SLEEP?

WHY CAN'T YOU BRING YOURSELF TO DO THAT ONE THING THAT YOU'D LOVE TO DO?

WHAT DO YOU WISH SOMEONE ELSE WOULD FINALLY SAY?

IF THE WORLD SUDDENLY HAD ACCESS TO ALL YOUR PAST THOUGHTS AND YOU COULD ONLY LOCK UP 5 OF THEM, WHICH WOULD THEY BE?

WHICH CRIMINALS DO YOU SECRETLY ROOT FOR?

IF YOU COULD ONLY GIVE YOUR TEENAGE SELF ONE BIT OF ADVICE, WHAT WOULD IT BE?

IF YOUR 8-YEAR-OLD SELF MET YOU TODAY, WHAT WOULD HE/SHE THINK OF YOU?

WHICH PERSON DO YOU DREAM ABOUT THE MOST?

WHAT WAS THE LAST THOUGHT YOU HAD THAT SCARED YOU?

WHAT FEELINGS DO YOU HAVE THAT YOU THINK ARE STUPID?

WHEN WAS THE LAST TIME YOU FORCED YOURSELF NOT TO CRY?

WHO IS COMPLETELY WRONG ABOUT YOU?

WHEN WAS THE LAST TIME YOU FELT HAPPY OVER SOMETHING SILLY?

WHAT DO YOU DO FOR NO OTHER REASON THAN VANITY?

WHAT DO YOU DO TO MAKE OTHER PEOPLE LIKE YOU?

WHO MAKES YOU JEALOUS?

IF YOU COULD SAY ONE SENTENCE THAT THE ENTIRE WORLD COULD HEAR, WHAT WOULD THAT SENTENCE BE?

WHEN WAS THE LAST TIME YOU SMILED BECAUSE YOU DID SOMETHING WRONG?

WHEN WAS THE LAST TIME YOU FELT ANGRY AND DIDN'T KNOW WHY?

WHEN ARE YOU TOO EASY ON YOURSELF?

WHEN DO YOU FIND YOURSELF FEELING UNGRATEFUL?

WHAT IS A COMMON THING THAT PEOPLE SAY THAT DRIVES YOU INSANE?

WHEN WAS THE LAST TIME YOU ACTED UNREASONABLY SELFISH?

WHAT DOES IT FEEL LIKE TO AGE?

WOULD YOU LIKE YOURSELF IF YOU WEREN'T YOU?

WHAT IS THE MOST EMBARRASSING THING YOU CONSISTENTLY DO?

WHAT WAS THE LAST MOMENT YOU WANTED TO LIVE IN FOREVER?

WHEN WAS THE LAST TIME YOU FELT LIKE A SLOB?

IF YOU WERE A SURREALIST, HOW WOULD YOU PAINT YOURSELF?

WHAT ARE YOU UNREASONABLY AFRAID OF?

WHEN WAS THE LAST TIME YOU FELT SMARTER THAN EVERYONE ELSE IN THE ROOM?

WHAT WAS THE LAST THOUGHT YOU HAD THAT SHOCKED YOURSELF?

WHAT IS THE DUMBEST THING YOU DO?

WHAT DO YOU DO WHEN YOU FEEL LONELY?

HOW DO YOU REACT INTERNALLY WHEN SOMEONE INSULTS YOU?

HOW DO YOU MAKE YOURSELF FEEL BETTER WHEN YOU'RE SCARED?

WHEN WAS THE LAST TIME YOU WERE SHAKING BECAUSE YOU WERE SO ANGRY?

WHEN WAS THE LAST TIME YOU WERE DISAPPOINTED?

HOW DO YOU FEEL WHEN SOMEONE PEEKS OVER YOUR SHOULDER WHEN YOU'RE READING?

WHEN WAS THE LAST TIME YOU COULDN'T BELIEVE WHAT YOU WERE SEEING?

WHAT IS THE WACKIEST THING YOU BELIEVE?

WHEN WAS THE LAST TIME YOU FELT BETTER THAN EVERYONE ELSE?

WHAT DO YOU NEED THAT'S COMPLETELY UNREASONABLE?

WHEN WAS THE LAST TIME YOU SHOULD HAVE FELT GUILTY, BUT DIDN'T?

WHEN WAS THE LAST TIME YOU WERE NERVOUS?

WHAT DO YOU TELL YOURSELF WHEN YOU'RE NERVOUS?

WHAT DO YOU WISH A STRANGER IN THE SEAT NEXT TO YOU ON A PLANE WOULD TELL YOU?

WHO WAS THE LAST PERSON YOU COULDN'T STOP STARING AT?

HOW DO YOU FEEL WHEN SOMEONE YOU DON'T LIKE CALLS YOU?

WHEN WAS THE LAST TIME YOU FELT DISGUSTED WITH YOURSELF?

AT WHAT AGE WERE YOU THE BEST VERSION OF YOURSELF?

WHEN WAS THE LAST TIME YOU FELT LIKE A GENIUS?

WHEN WAS THE LAST TIME YOU FELT LIKE AN IDIOT?

WHEN WAS THE LAST TIME YOU KNEW SOMETHING THEY DIDN'T KNOW?

HOW DO YOU FEEL WHEN SOMEONE COMPLIMENTS YOU?

HOW DO YOU FEEL WHEN YOU DON'T KNOW THE WORD SOMEONE JUST USED?

IF YOU WERE AN UNLIKEABLE CHARACTER IN A BOOK, HOW WOULD THE AUTHOR DESCRIBE YOU?

IF YOU WERE A LIKEABLE CHARACTER IN A BOOK, HOW WOULD THE AUTHOR DESCRIBE YOU?

HOW DOES IT FEEL WHEN SOMETHING GOOD HAPPENS TO SOMEONE YOU DON'T LIKE?

WHEN WAS THE LAST TIME YOU SAID SOMETHING NASTY TO SOMEONE YOU LOVE?

HOW IS ADULTHOOD DIFFERENT FROM WHAT YOU EXPECTED AS A CHILD?

WHEN WAS THE LAST TIME YOU AMAZED YOURSELF?

WHAT IS A GOOD QUALITY THAT OTHERS THINK YOU POSSESS, THAT YOU DON'T ACTUALLY POSSESS?

HOW DO YOU FEEL AFTER YOU BUY SOMETHING EXPENSIVE?

WHEN WAS THE LAST TIME YOU SAID THE OPPOSITE OF WHAT YOU WERE THINKING?

WHEN WAS THE LAST TIME YOU BECAME ANGRY WITH SOMEONE FOR DOING SOMETHING THAT YOU OFTEN DO?

WHAT ARE YOU MOST AFRAID TO SAY?

"FOR MYSELF, FOR A LONG TIME... MAYBE I FELT INAUTHENTIC OR SOMETHING, I FELT LIKE MY VOICE WASN'T WORTH HEARING, AND I THINK EVERYONE'S VOICE IS WORTH HEARING. SO IF YOU'VE GOT SOMETHING TO SAY, SAY IT FROM THE ROOFTOPS."

- TOM HIDDLESTON